# Nowhere Near Moloka'i

# Nowhere Near Moloka'i

乱

Gary Chang

Bear Star Press
2004

NOWHERE NEAR MOLOKA'I
© 2004 by Gary Chang
All Rights Reserved

Printed in the United States of America
10 9 8 7 6 5 4 3 2 1

BEAR STAR PRESS
185 Hollow Oak Dr.
Cohasset, CA 95973
530.891.0360
*www.bearstarpress.com*


Cover design: Text Plus Now / Pat Matsueda
Cover photo courtesy of Keith Yabusaki
Book design: Beth Spencer


ISBN: 0-9719607-3-9
Library of Congress Control Number: 2003111158

# Table of Contents

*For all the braddahs and sistahs*

# How Greydog Picked Up His Name

## TIGER: AN 'AUMĀKUA FEEDS

East Maui – and the mist pauses
over Keʻanae Bay.
Its mottled shell
amber in the converging light,
a young *honu* breaks the sea's surface.

The lone sooty tern glides slowly
near the edge of the bay. As the sky clears it lifts
broad-surfaced wings
and cries.

Slight but definite,
the water quickens.
A fin-tip slashes out of the sea,
veers and vanishes. The tern
   continues to shriek.

Unable to see on the surface,
the turtle descends
into colder blue waters. It strokes
powerfully, casting no shadow.

          With no sound,
*manō* accelerates off the ocean floor, angling
hard for the unprotected belly. Sunlight
flashes across her back.

    Black eyes fixed on
the turtle's crooked flipper, death
drops her lower jaw, stiffens her pectoral fins
and with a flick of her tail,
     takes the offering.

## HOMECOMING

Mother Ocean rock our cradle.
We follow the stars.
Sister whale and dolphin
Sing eternal. Come
Shark – *'Aumākua* – protect us.
Voyage and discover.

## BROKEN PIES

> *… but once they smash there is no way to put them right.*
> Louise Erdrich, *Love Medicine*

*Hapai* Nani wears the purple
badge of aloha, unsure
who is the father. Sleep
my Prince Valium.

Development costs
measured in grams. Cowboy
rides the wind on payday,
body fixed, spirit broken.

*Pau hana*, drink *mana*
six-pack, twelve, was it
a case? Lost count,
gained understanding

of a seething anger
whirling spirals. Next morning:
A sober moment, drunk with pain.
The anger shares my face.

*Hōkūle'a*, Orion, Pleiades,
where are your voyagers?
Guide them; they wander
dreaming of stars.

I vainly rage at you,
God; please forgive me.
Afraid to fade away.
Unremembered.

## How Greydog Picked up His Name

Old Man sputters awake, forcing breath
through lungs clogged like an abused
air filter. His fingers, often bent
into arthritic claws, thankfully creak
in obedience.
                    Of his seventy-three years,
he has worked forty at Universal Motors, doing,
among other things, a hundred too many
brake jobs.

                    As he has done for the past
twenty-four years, he will celebrate this opening day
of Hawai'i's game bird season on Moloka'i.
                    In his youth, he hunted
pheasants above where Kahala
Mall now stands and shot doves flying
over a chicken farm
that would later

                    become Kalani High School.
The hunt this November morning
will be the first Old Man and Grey will share.
                    Although he occasionally
calls Grey "Boy," the fact
that at twenty-three he is Old Man's
junior is incidental.

                    Old Man watches
Grey with the amusement he awards
puppies. Seeing Grey hurdle the condo
furniture at 4:30, however,
he sits up on the bed.

                    "How goes it, Old Man?"

Old Man shakes his head,
says:
                    *If you don't slow down, Grey,*
                    *you're gonna kill me.*

## Grey Confides to Joker the Labrador About Old Man

Pre-dawn on West Moloka'i: light without
light, the sky black, pregnant with stars.
The half-moon prisms in the surf, tiny
droplets of light thrown off
in the shorebreak.

Grey steps out of the condo.
No headlights yet appear on the low hills. Sticking
his hands into the pockets of his vest, Grey hurries
to Old Man's Ford, a four-by-four half-ton
painted fire engine yellow.
        Secured to the truck's black tubular
rollbar is the eighty-pound Labrador named Joker.

Joker stands: even before he hears Grey's footsteps,
he knows him by his scent. Through square
jowls, the Labrador breathes deep; his chest
expands, filled with vitality. Other than his ivory
teeth and a slight silver feathering beneath his thick tail,
Joker is completely black.

    *Yo! Mutthead,*
*good morning.*

Joker springs up and down.
When he lands, he spreads and collapses
his front legs, coiled like a sprinter
in the bed of the truck.

    *Hush.*
Grey grabs his cheeks,
pulls the dog's face toward his own. Joker snorts, then licks
Grey on the mouth.

*Damn, Dog!*
*How many times I gotta tell you:*
                    *'No lips.'*


Grey spits, sits on the tailgate.
                        The Lab prances.


        *Joker, sit.*
                    He looks at Grey.


Grey stares back,
repeats the command:
                        *Sit!*


        Joker slowly drops
his rear end onto the truck bed.
His tail quivers.


        *Good boy.*
The tail picks up tempo; Joker
regards Grey,
                    grins.


*Old Man would scold you.*
*He already went scold me.*


The Labrador attempts to lever his head under
Grey's arm. His tongue hangs out
the side of his mouth.


            *But us two braddahs,*
*we get 'em. We go sit here, talk stink*
            *'bout Old Man.*
Joker stands,
tail clanking the truck bed wall.
Grey wrestles him into a headlock.


        *Okay, okay: I talk.*
            *You stink.*

Grey releases the Lab.
Joker tries to stand but Grey holds him
down by the ears.
        Grey jumps off the truck;
Joker crouches, prepared for the next attack.
Unhooking the stay from the dog's collar, Grey takes
two steps away from the truck
and pats his leg:
          *Joker, heel.*


      The Labrador pounces off the truck.
He sits left of his new master,
          tail still flailing.

# Lāna'i after the Pineapple
*for Paul Chun*

Just inside the plate glass window I meet Old Man.
Although the settlement store
has replaced its interior lights with fluorescent tubes,
the outside lamp remains incandescent
and it flickers. A pile of discarded clothes
lies heaped at the bottom of the wooden
stairs. As we exit *Hea and Now*, Old Man stops
next to the pile and says,
                    "Good morning, Pablo."

Without standing, Pablo lifts his face and broken
grin into the hesitant light. A dark blue
bandanna circles his forehead. Parched
and creased from a lifetime
of exposure, his skin stretches impossibly over his stick body
like a hand-me-down several sizes too small.
He has the scarred hands
of a pineapple picker. Soiled
red and holey beyond repair, his jeans expose legs
pricked by the crowns.
                    From the back of his mouth, Pablo
rolls out a glowing *Toscani* cigar on his tongue. From the
shadows, he produces a bottle filled with a dark liquid;
holds the bottle up
to Old Man's belly: *Salut, Padre.*

Old Man turns to the cane break
fluttering in the breeze. A rooster crackles
in the rose of dawn's arrival;
                    "Little too early, *Manong.*"

Pablo mock-studies his watch.
He grins, *No, I think almost too late.*

"Take care, Pablo."

Old Man and I start for the truck.
Pablo has already tucked his head
back into the army jacket's collar;
once again, he disappears.

"Klingon cloaking device," I explain.

"They've got
to fix that
lamp," says Old Man,
his voice barely heard over the rooster
celebrating the new day.

# HOUSE OF THE SUN

亂

# Orpheus Descends into the House of the Sun

*Forget your song, ignore it. It will end.*
*True singing needs a very different breath.*
*An airless breath. A breath within the god. A wind.*
Rilke, *The Sonnets to Orpheus: I,3*

I guard the funnel where the western ridge of Haleakalā
becomes the west border of Kaupo Gap. Behind the rim
the sun sinks. The twelve
goats on the inside face of the wall, fleeing the lone driver,
appear like phantoms. They avoid the fence that encircles
the crater rim higher up. One hundred sixty yards above,
an old nanny sees me lift my rifle.
In the dying light my extra bullets gleam
like ancient gold.

*Among the light dead I take my position.*

Kona winds – ash from Kilauea – bend
the *pūkiawe* shrub beside me, touch my face.
The Winchester recoils off my shoulder,
off my cheek, again and again.

*Orpheus grieves; but the furies*
*rage deeper still.*

His intestines corded
around the nanny's foreleg, the billy blocks escape. He cries
but can go nowhere. I shoot the *keiki* two goats behind him.
The kid rebounds
off the wall and falls, bleating, eyes wide.
It flails its legs
like they were wings but cannot resist
death's terrific pull.

*In silence, I listen to the crystal*
*shatter even as it rings.*

Only the disemboweled billy remains
alive. He stares at his stomach
streaming out behind the nanny, my last victim.
Drawn, the billy presents
a smaller target.

The concussion his carcass makes on
the crater floor sounds like the thunderbolt
I cast from my hands.

*Thirteen years from now
his song will still be mine,
powdered glass in my blood.*

Alone on a crag on the east rim
of the House of the Sun. Haleakalā.
Outside the lip, a cloud, black and heavy,
approaches fast. I hear air
seeping out of a tire – but there are no cars
at this altitude. Mauna Kea looks me in the eye.

Again the hiss. Faint and low.

A National Park Service hired gun, I track the leak. I'd rather
eat my lunch; instead I find her behind smooth rocks.

From twelve feet away, the goat looks like Fear,
my black Labrador, sleeping. Inhale: chest expands so smooth.

Exhale: bright red froth bubbles
from a puncture behind her left foreleg,
lung shot. Oxygen-rich bright life pulses along
her black coat. Then clots

darker, matted like night coming on.

Another bubble. Black pestilence
shatters it.
Huge blue-green eyes, iridescent gems hung
on my Christmas tree.

Wings buzz erratic, wet and audible –
blood specks the wind. The horsefly drinks
the sweet air, calls its brothers and into the sweeter fountain
dives again. Amazed
my hand follows its flight, touches the deflated

hide. Suddenly, the nanny wakes, lifts her head
and bleats
nearly voiceless; her blood spurts
louder. I find my hand has clenched

my unsheathed blade; my weak hand reaches
for her cheek. She does not resist. A swarm of flies
rushes in to nurse.

My blade waves goodbye.
*Ee-oh, ee-oh.*

I shoot four goats off Haleakalā's east inside rim,
record these kills in my National Park
Service log.

        Half a mile from the tent I share
with Alan, a goat's severed
head rests on a rock. Horseflies exit
the bloody mouth, a puck-
sized stone wedged in. Another swarm
works its neck bone.

        Flies cling to my arm,
sticky. I break the rock free, hurl it over the *pali* –
other rocks clatter
away.
        Flies reenter, light
on the goat's tongue.

        Where you hiding, Butcherman?

        I scout the *'ama'u* ferns
fifty yards downslope for the animal's body. Nothing.
Not a track.

        I return to the head. My right hand touches
cinder, gravel sticks to the stain on my palm.

        From behind the *māmane* tree,
from behind my eyes, he watches me. What's
        the punch line, Alan?

I wipe my palm on the black forehead,
worse the blood smears.

Horseflies buzz my face again.

        My laughter joins their whir,
        just short of.

## Alan Enters the Campsite
## in Darkness

A nanny bawls a quarter mile away from the valley
south. Fifteen minutes later
a shorter bleat followed by a shot confirms the kid
has found its mother one
       last time. I wait to hear

           the second shot but none
comes. Half an hour later the wounded nanny still cries.

Alan approaches me. He spits
on the cinder, smirks
        *You see my goat's head, Grey?*

"Yup, can't miss it."
        *Figured these stupid things*
       *would catch the hint. Stay the fuck*
         *out of here.*

"Alan, what's happening down there? The nanny's
been crying for nearly an hour."
        *We baited the keiki back.*
        *Finally got him.*

"Yeah, I heard the shot. But why
didn't someone kill the mother?" Alan puts his hand
       on my shoulder.

   *That's the sound of the forest regenerating itself.*

       I try to look at Alan's face
but the sun has already sunk below the crater rim.
He withdraws his hand.

      The nanny lasts until a little before eleven. After she
quiets, only Alan's snoring disturbs the tent.

# Under the Winter Moon

When the blue cold of evening
blankets the crater, the holy light,
*la'a kea*, comes. I return
to the rim and sit
with my palms together.

Kaupo wind rises
like the breath from a tomb
and sweeps over the bodies scattered
across the lava below. These animals
quiver but when the air stills
they die again;
their moonlit eyes seem to search the jagged rock.

      Song rings through the night, penetrates
the edge of my dream;
*nēnē* geese in flight, strong voices
in this lonely place.

      Dawn has not yet risen when I step out
from my tent. Stars fill the heavy
sky and the wind pours
into me. I reach
for the geese and they soar
unbowed high above.
A mongoose scraps
for flesh in a forest regrowing itself.

# SINGER


*for Pat, her sister*

We sat on the mountain,
you and I,
children of indifferent gods.
You sang the dawn gold and magenta,
like a phoenix across the gray sky.
I listened horrified
when you talked
to the voices in your head. You ran
Kalanianaole Highway, dodging
cars and illness that sought
your beauty like bullets.

Alone, I wait on this crag
in a sky dark and oppressive.
Come home, Kathleen.
I never told you
how beautifully you sing.

# WHEN GODS DIE

You called it the Void, Old Man.
Hidden darkness
like the shattered bodies of beasts
on the rim of the House of the Sun. Lightning
ripped the sky, sundered stone in a storm too beautiful
for man. The scorched air smoked with copper.

                                                            I witnessed
wrath that night. Small and alone, I cried with my rifle
while chaos raged outside.
                                        *Come home, Grey*, you said.

So I left the gut-shot nanny on the ledge,
she unwilling to lean forward
to free-fall, death; and I,
I returned to an illusion, those who pretended
tolerance. Then, your own blood
killed you.
                                 *I'll always love you, Son.*
You looked weak.
                         *Take care.*

A day before your natural-born kids cremated
your body, I saw you.

                                I would have said,
                                      "God rest your soul."

But in Haleakalā Crater
you and I had already destroyed our gods.
You returned there
in an ambulance, bleeding from another
blood infection,
crying,
                 *Shoot me.*

Your daughter shied away, unwilling to touch you.

                      Last night the rat trap shattered
another life. A black streak, Fear beat
me to it. The rat squealed, its back leg twisted
and obscene. Fear
devoured the pain as if it were his alone.
                             "Good boy, drop it."

What remained
I dumped into the outside rubbish can.

Fear and I walk to Thomas Square,
October night, step into the silence. Outside the public
restroom, where the light
ends, druggies harass the homeless.
                   *So what's new? Packs always*
*prey near the fringe.* They approach the fresh
meat. I've no handgun.
Fear bristles.

At home, unable to speak, I oil your rifle. So
slick. I leave the Springfield out
next to the bed as exhaustion overcomes me.
Wake up at 4:00 this morning. Fear
still grins.
I clutch your .30-06. Something
touched my sleep:
                   *Come home, Grey.*

Is that you, Old Man?

# BROKEN 'OHANA

## GREY SECEDES WITH A CASE OF MOOSEHEAD

> *... and my fists*
> *will sing songs of forgiveness*
> Adrian C. Louis, *This is No Movie of Noble Savages*

The company paid $7,000 for Big Texas Red,
a ninety-pound chocolate Lab
from a champion line.
He attacked horses, knocked down
*keiki* and even urinated on the cowboys.
If a dog could be *haole*, Big Texas
Red was *nui haole*.


Kipahulu Ranch paid me $2,000 per month
plus lodging and tips to guide
those Great White Hunters
whose memsahib desired me
inflate her little sahib,
> "*Hala*! Great shot, Macomber."


Big Texas Red came with the job description.
Three weeks after I arrived, Red sat, stayed,
came, heeled, fetched
on command and obeyed *no* and *drop it*
most of the time.


He still sprayed the unwary.


Two weeks later, Red and I hunted a field of *kikiyu* grass.
On the pasture's edge, Spanish moss dangled
from a *kukui* nut tree. The tree's fallen seed
thickened the air with mold.


> Suddenly, a pheasant
cock erupted out of the *kukui*'s trunk.
> *Kaboom!*
> The cock tumbled into a scrub
of thorny Hawaiian poppies. Its iridescent
feathers shimmered.

                    Big Texas Red never stopped.
*Red! You damned shit, stay!*
*Come!*


I retrieved Red. Persuaded him over the *kolohala*.


*Red! Dead bird.*
          He sniffed the pheasant, licked
its wing, stepped forward,
                    *Fetch it!*
          raised his rear leg.


So I cracked him fast, hard in the throat.
Which scared the piss out of Big Texas Red.
Spasms seized his legs, then spread
until even his tongue jerked.


I picked up the pheasant and walked back
to the ranch headquarters.


*Pau hana* an hour later.


          Peter and Junior-Boy swing
lathered saddles over the wooden feed trough.
Curried and full of grain, their quarter horses whinny
from pasture. The two *paniola* join me
in bullshit. On the third round of Mooseheads,
Peter regards the empty kennel.
                    "Red?"

*Futthead scared for come home.*


He sucks another Moosehead, smiles
too loud. Junior-Boy yanks on his drink
as if he holds reins:
"Whoa the fuck down, little pony."

We *kani* our bottles:
One more beer to the tough guy wannabe.
One more beer to every *braddah* he'd ever pissed on.
One more beer to that pig-headed maggot squirming
in the *puakala* nettles.

One more beer, one more
case, one more shitfaced drunk
to Big Texas Red.
       Every single damned one of them.

# FEAR SEEKS ANOTHER

After the attack
the newborn calf looks like a jigsaw puzzle missing
major pieces. Flies
feed on the nearly dead animal.

Several mutilated but uneaten
hen pheasants – toys broken by a child's tantrum – will
clutch eggs no more. Fear's tail twitches
at half mast; he glances frequently
my way.

What began as a nuisance of dogs abandoned by
poachers evolved into a feral pack of hunters
savaging the ranch's livestock. Until some social
scientist utilized the term *wilding,* from *A Clock-
work Orange,* it was called pack behavior.

Before harsher methods are employed, the
managers of Kipahulu Ranch decide to shoot
those dogs careless enough to be caught in the
open and then trap the few that have escaped the
rifles. Animals captured in the wire cages would
be *euthanized.*

Grey Chen, the ranch's Professional Hunter,
would execute the plan.

To verify the other dogs' tracks seems
pointless. Fear licks the blood
off the grass. I do not
stop him; meat
is meat.
Standing three feet behind
the wheezing calf's head, I suck in my breath
and draw my pistol.

Fear returns to me before the shot.

# Hunted Animals

*… the snout filled with silence and slime
and vendetta was born.*
          Pablo Neruda, *"The Dictators"*

Bud and I approach the Humane Society trap
located *mauka* of the guava trees in paddock 41,
where the pack last preyed.
We hear no birds.

He is built like a Brittany Spaniel
and has the breed's liver-on-white colors.
No more than two years old, he weighs
about forty pounds.
Shit clings to his left haunch.

"Still better than lacing strychnine,
          Bud. At least
     he isn't wearing a collar."

     The dog crouches
away from us, flattens his ears
and barks.

I snap the clip into the .22.
Bud pulls on his leather gloves, swings
the restraint rod.

          The dog growls when we near the trap.
He attacks Bud and me
through the cage. The metal
stops his teeth.

"Now he's really pissed,"
          smirks Bud,
     "all over the place."

I move to the rear of the cage; the animal
shadows, snapping.
Bud opens the trap's door,
threads the rod through the crack.
                              "Gotcha."

Saliva froths.
              *This is cruel, Bud, get him out.*
              I load the rifle.
                              *Snick.*

"No problem,
              make like bait."

I stand in front of the trap.
When Buddy kicks open the wire door
the dog lunges for my thigh.
Bud yanks him away.

                    The dog snarls,
bites his own lip. Spits blood.

Bud bends the animal.
I steady the rifle's muzzle
against its skull:
Teeth stop clacking at the shot.
                              *Snick.*

              I set the muzzle
above the dog's right ear, squeeze off
                        another shot;
his flesh deflates.
Only the animal's gurgling disturbs the quiet.

*Buddy, no stink up the car,*
            *tie him to the bumper.*
*His drag will attract the other pigs.*

Bud does not meet my eyes.

                        I drive slowly
to a nearby depression. Buddy exits
before I can open my door,
heaves the carcass into the gulch.

Bud returns.

"Uncle, the *pua'a* will eat
            him tonight.
Nobody going know what went happen."

We drive back to the ranch headquarters,
that silence particular to violence
settling on the pasture.

# GREY POACHES ONE *PUA'A* FOR THE KOUS

My hunters exit their vehicles near the *makai*
edge of paddock 39. In the early morning mist
they appear
unshaven, in dark stained fatigues.
          *Ku'e akena* of previous hunts.

Their leader sets down his Marlin lever rifle,
barrel splotched, no longer blue. Callused and scarred,
his right hand brandishes one kitchen knife, long
with plenty belly. He says
to Keoni, his nine-year-old son:
          *And this stay how you hemo*
          *his heart,*

but he looks at me.

          Keoni shifts from one
foot to attention,
smiles in the sea breeze.

I nod from his father, Hayden,
down to him,
          *not so hard*
smile.

I take the Winchester out the Isuzu,
sling it over my shoulder. Look up
          *the father still stay*
*staring at me*

to the *pu'u*
we going climb. I swipe my hands against my
jeans. Licking my lips, I grin
at Hayden:
          "You *braddahs* ready?"

34

## Ranch Headquarters: Fear Runs Black in the Night and I Run with Him

Ehu stinks of piss.

I grip the gun tight
like dancing with Maile,
whose husband slams my icebox
fucked up on coke and sex
soon to be inflicted.
Ehu menaces his flashlight.

Fear exits the shadows
snarling,
yellow canines specked with foam.
Mid-leap: time stands still

but lands deeper
in the shade;
an old Lab mean and white.

> *Damn fuck*
hurts my ears.
Maile beat purple tomorrow;
> pretty Maile, *hapai* Maile.
The revolver feels good in my hand.

> *Get your fuckin' dog out my face,*

"Fear, down,"
> I command.

> *before I kill him.*

Ehu glares at Fear
so intent
he does not see me
wrestle the trigger.

No one else here, Ehudick.

Fear stares me in the eye.
   "Fear. Down!"
*Baby. . .*

I kneel on the tiles,
stroke the beast
So soft.

   *I going fuck your dog.*

Ehu sees death in my hand.

   "No more, Ehu,"
            small voice
sounds like me.

Ehu cries like one *keiki,*
Fear slips back into night, looking
more and more a part of it.

I hear sirens: *Ehu broke in
                  went psycho.*

Morning rises hard,
Maile wears shades.

## To the Blue-Eyed Gentleman
## Who Lectured Me About Hegemony While
## I Played Fetch with Fear

Dawn rose in Makiki out of the twilight
you escaped. I smiled, lowered my eyes

to the seven goats I had shattered that afternoon,
their bones and entrails sprayed
across Haleakalā in bloody fans, no longer
*a threat to indigenous life forms.*

I slung the rifle over my shoulder: I was out of
bullets but my knife was
sharp. I used to cry like those

crippled bodies watching me descend, tripping
so ungoatlike. I unsheathed
the blade and my fingers trembled;
how effortlessly the five-inch sliver pierced

the nanny's neck. Sliced through hair,
skin and textures I could not name
before her nearly severed head

rebounded off the stained earth. Finished, I attended to her kid.
The small one was not really
worth the effort but there were no
others and I was still so hungry.

Yet, I had known no prejudice until this morning
when you came, Whiteman
with the *haole* mind. You hissed,
*Chink, why don't you go back to Gooksville.*

Please, please, please stop, my hands are tingling.

# COMING TO COLO

And then,
Braddah Goose, nighttime you still wear your lava-lava?
Or now too cold, freeze them gonads? For real, Kupau, how
stay your *'ōpū*, still pushing four hundred pounds? You and
        Nick better slack key those spam *musubi.*
Pissed off no more *bento* here. Even you tell them give you
one plate lunch they look you like you *pupule.* Gonzo:
fifteen pounds the last nine weeks. But I stay more mellow
        from the last time I went write.


                *Pau* workshop last Wednesday,
some *kāne* took me go suck choke beer. Had one Korean
*tita* with us from upside Michigan – her name Cheyenne –
but over here she stay *Asian.* Over here no more Koreans,
like you no can say,
            "You *hapa-haole*, or
                    what?"


Little while I start *wala'au pidgin*, telling them
about Nick's *No Pau Kau-Kau Halau.*
                But Cheyenne,
        she no understand.
        "What does *kau-kau* mean?" she says.


        "*Kau-kau* is 'to eat' and *halau* is 'one school' so
*No Pau Kau-Kau Halau* means "The School That Never
Finishes Eating."
                And then she catch
                *Hui 'o Microwave.*
        "Fuckin' A," she says.


Thirty-four degrees, no more gloves and we stay outside
*kani* Honey Lager.


                Rolling, I tell you
                    Kupau, rolling
            on the sidewalk.

I max out at seventy, nowhere near sober,
southbound in the left lane of 287. The street
lights end, the chassis lifts with the wind.
                                    I turn off my headlights,
speed into the Fossil Creek depression.


                                    *Mama told me
                    when I was young, Come sit beside me
                                    my only son.*


                                    *Hōkūle'a*, the home star
sputters and flares, yellow lane marker glitters
through snow.
                    Here
between old blood and the rush of new
ambition, for that instant between frost and memory,
booming through with no gravity in this blue
broke-door Suzuki.


                                    *You can do this, if you try,
                    all I want for you is be satisfied.
                                    Be a simple man.*


                    The lights of the oncoming cars,
celestial candles of the *obon*, festival
for the dead, float down the Ala Wai Canal.

Flash me.

## I Shop Safeway When I Need
## one Attitude

Yo, Budhead,

I went drive Lois-Ann to Denver International
this morning so she should get home pretty soon.
You no can believe how sweet was for *wala'au*, even if
Lois-Ann like for make trouble. Last night, we all stay
waiting for dinner, and the *kolohe* asks me, "So why you
stay here, never get accepted West Coast?"
Talk about make-A.
When *sistah* talk I like cry.

Back home, you remember how when you use the Safeway
card the cashiers go read your name on the receipt?
*Thank you for shopping Safeway,*
*Mr. Chien.*

And I would scold them, "Eh, no call me that. Make me
feel so damned old." Then they like laugh — plenty of them
know me from dig-nose days.

At the checkout this morning, the *braddah* in front me get
one blond ponytail, stay chanting. More worse, he smelled
*hauna*, like he never went bathe. *Braddah* paid up.
*Have a good day, Mr. Engle,*
she told him.

Come my turn, I like talk story but the cashier no can look
my eyes.

And when she give me back my change, she still no say shit.
Only put the money on the counter. My name right there
on the receipt, Kupau.          For real, I went check.

I wanted for go scold the manager.

But that's so fuckin' *haole.*

## To Video a Waterfall
## You and Your Dad Drive Four Hours
## This Sunday Afternoon

Distressed train whistles through the storm. Flash flood
watch issued for east-central Colorado.
"Where's Rifle?"

*Southwest of Fort Collins,*
you said.

An echo in my dream wakes me. Black rain
still falls on the roof, bird shit stains the front window. Only
Fear tethers me to this empty bed. His paws echo
down a silent hall.

In your room I stand upright the silk
letters of your name; Fear sniffs the rabbit doll again. For
two days more
we pace this house alone.

I flick on the outside lamp, stagger up the darkened stairs
and wait for sleep.

You prose like an inexperienced lover
in the poet's embrace.
He knows something,
peers into your face.
Touching your skin,
he abandons you and grieves:
the white space
of your rewrites seems like great chunks of his body,
facts your mind believes.

You and I are children in red dresses
snatching cactus from the prairie,
following the faces of other children
with our fingers,
watching words
fly from mouth to mouth.

I even talk like them.

Yup, choked with *haoles*.
Roommate no lock the front door, leave his dishes in the
sink for days, even when he frickin' out-of-state. I put one
rubbish can under the sink but he rather dump his *opala*
in his box on the floor. Fear *grinds* the Haagen Daaz out
the box; see how he runs.

                    Hegemony no can even say *mahalo*.

                        Stay some hard for aloha.

Couple English profs, Dundee and Uma Sue (two first
names), took me hiking this weekend up Lory State Park.
As Dundee walked past it, this snake coiled and rattled.
When stay only four feet from your leg, one timber rattler
can flick plenty stink-eye. And yeah, they get forked
tongues. Black like plague.

We never kill the snake. I had my blade, lots of dead
branches on the ground.
But I went *mana'o* my friends.
                        *Fear, down.*

Dundee commanded, "Shoo, snake," until it slid under
a rock.
                  I really wanted to. Hope
          nobody got struck.

*A hui ho kako*, Budhead. Take care.

Old Man would tell you, "If you have to cry, no more
shame."

You know what I mean.
*Kani* one Moosehead for me.

                  *Bumbye pau,*
                  Greydog

## Please Send the "No Touch the Native" T-Shirt

Matsushige-san:

Remember one time I broke up with Avis and you and me
went drink big-time at Ala Mo? We sucked the Mickeys,
then whacked the bottle vodka. Pretty soon the two liters
Mountain Dew *gonzo,* but we stay singing.
 Then we checked out the Korean bar. The stuff
that *wahine* could do with the cigar, no can believe.

 Or how about the Thanksgiving we went camp
inside Haleakalā. I carried three gallons water and the tent,
forgot one pole. You humped in two days *grinds*, no
bird, but you donated the bottle Wild Turkey.
 Clouds went roll into the crater that night: thirty
degrees, *māmane* trees stay *huli* in the wind and everything
look like slate. Nobody could sleep when inside the tent got
choked wet.

You still remember how the dark<br>
rumped petrel – 'uwa'u – cried?

Kue, kue.

"Only on Maui," you told me, "one Chinaman can go shoot
goats on his birthday, especially when stay Federal Holiday."

Early Tuesday morning, 7:20, I wait for the xerox machine
warm up, for copy "Keeping Close to Home." Snow
swirling outside, just like the movies, one gray cloud on
top the Eddy Building. This professor come talk story, puts
down his cup coffee. His left hand *pili* my shoulder, then he
smiles, "It's good to include such diversity in the teaching
of Freshman Comp."
I figure one camera going pop out the machine.

Guarans-ballbarans, Curtis,
we going need more than one case.

48

## *BACHI:* POEM FOR A MANEATER

### 1. BAD FOR BUSINESS

*The shark took out a "big chunk" of Knutson's thigh and
she was bleeding profusely as* [boyfriend Bruce C. Brown]
*swam, pulling her toward shore. Knutson passed out along
the way. Gemini Capt. J. Dushane said, "The side of the leg
was gone. There was just this big gaping hole. It was
unfortunate."*

*The attack between 11:00 and 11:30 a.m. prompted state
officials to post signs warning beach-goers to stay out of
the water along a one-mile section of the resort. Operators
of ocean tours and activities say business was slow because
of the warning.*

### 2. CAPTAIN AHAB AT SIX

Till Daddy walked in, smacked me,
                    "*Bakatare,* you like
            broke your leg? *Bachi* for play
            with your grandmother's cane."

snatched back my wooden leg.
                    "What you crying for?
            I'll give you one reason to cry."

Returned to me *Babang's* cane.

**3.** **OFFICIALS CLOSE MAUI SHARK-ATTACK SITE**

> *The Maui woman who was attacked*
> *near Kaanapali is in guarded*
> *condition after surgery*
> read the *Star-Bulletin* headline,

impersonal, vulgar
like the postcard
you've tacked to the department
bulletin board
as a joke: a Great White rends the bait, jaws
grotesque. Membrane shields her eyes and flesh runs
from her teeth. Beneath the picture,
the caption reads:

> *Send more tourists . . .*

Hawai'i

# FACE

# This Aloha We Write One Another

Flat Cat quit the program, gone
home to Michigan's little finger, to her sandy moraine
floating above Sutton's Bay and Leland.

> *Couldn't find a fit,*
> *she said.*

Sad-eyed and pregnant, she stole her lyrics
back to the Happy Hour Tavern, back to prickly
alfalfa, where pockets of black soil edge the dark
scat of glacial remains.

> "So how the fuck do I write
> now, S.J.?"

Paint Sunday in watercolors.
Forget the *-isms*. Remember those poems
stuffed inside letters only a dozen friends
will ever read.

> Two kestrels streak the rooftops,
alternating white and russet,
angle to curve; the smaller male strokes
against Newton's law,
climbing nearly
straight
up
a wall
of vertical freedom.

> Thirteen feet, eight wingbeats into
orbit, tucks in blue-gray wings and pauses
in freefall, a tiny form
unable to contain
such joy.

## Freckles Used to Scrap Fear
## for the Table

*Howzit, Kanak:*
Nick doing okay on dialysis? Please give her my
aloha. I know stay hard but you gotta hang on. Eh, you ever
talk *pidgin* by yourself, little while start make believe. But
not for real, like *musubi* without spam.
On my first day teaching Freshman Comp, I
wrote on the whiteboard, "The 'Jeopardy' answer is '*Non,
mais je parle un peu français.*'" Below this I wrote,
"The 'Jeopardy' question is 'Do you speak Chinese?'"
Cool head, *Cuz*, at least I never tell them, "Ah-Toto, lookee
like we not in Kansas no more."
Well, what I supposed to do? Maybe Fort
Collins no more *'ōhi'a lehua,* but if 15% of the world get
non-brown eyes, they all stay here. Blue eyes, cobalt eyes,
so damned many Conan the Barbarian eyes. *Hala!*
"English is a learning endeavor, not one ethnicity."

Laters, Budhead.
My mother called this weekend, asked
me how Fear was doing. *Nobody for watch TV
with nighttime so I go upstairs early. Sometimes
I go lie down on your bed, your old room, look
for you and the black dog. You no stay so I go
back your father's room sleep.*

Still the same back home. My sisters, all the time
they scold her. They no understand. After Freckles had
couple strokes, she no can – like before, yeah?
Not her fault my father went die on her
birthday.
*Boy, this the first time your father no stay home
eat with me today.*

Never have anything I could tell her
*You no miss me anymore, Grey?*

so I wrote these lines:

*SLIDE*
*I've lost a life*
*I can't remember*
*disappearing  My mind*

*grieves absent*
*Where*
*are the names?*

       Sometimes I scared, Kupau
          I going forget the names too.

## For Those Impure Words Not Selected

The audience claps for the gallery reader.
                              I see their hands.

I kill three goats on *Pu'u Māmane*,
approach the most easily
possessed carcass. Rifle on the cinder, I draw
my knife. When I touch the nanny,
I know she carries
*keiki.* The National Park considers a *hapai*
nanny a bonus.

I remove backstraps from her spine, careful
not to see her belly,
or the parting of flesh.
My knife slips through fur, slashes
the first joint of my index finger. Before the blade
completes its stroke, I feel it touch bone.
                              I watch, fascinated,
as my finger flashes
white, as if the finger itself
has fainted,
for that instant before the fatty tissue
opens
like torch ginger,
splashed with life.

The meat sack hangs
heavy off the pine. My face
gives its color to the sack.
Death blows bitter in my bones.

At Colorado State, the post-modern poet says I possess
*an aesthetic for death.*

I sleep under the damp pine.
Come sleep with me, come feel the air
shimmer around the meat sack.

                    Seek the blood on your white gloves.

## Captain Aloha Winkies
## for Prairie Dogs

Little Kapiko:

This morning, Captain Aloha called me up, gave me shit
about my prairie dog message: "*Braddah*," he asked, " why
you like shoot them fuzzballs?"

Cause I never stay home,
he went scold my voice-mail: "Someday, Grey, when you
spocking one dog-hole, I going pop out in my *lava-lava*.
Show you one effin'prairie dog."

While I calling him back, I *akamai* of when we went shoot
this rifle match. Captain, he lucked out, drew first squad.
Lying on his *opu*, he set up for shoot prone. Me and twenty
other *mahus*, we all standing behind him.
Now, Captain is one thick
Hawaiian: six feet, three hundred eighty pounds. Kinda
hard for him shoot prone, yeah, but nobody like laugh.
More worse, he get on his *lava-lava*, bright orange with
two yellow hibiscus, one humongous flower for each
cheek. He work construction, so Captain stay choke
*pāpaʻa*. But above his knees, white like one *haole*.
Eh, not like we like look, but
nobody had choice. And then, the *braddah*, he went spread
his legs. No can believe, K, underneath he stay naked.
Like in *Braveheart*, when Gibson's *braddahs* went moon
the English. I no shit you, his guavas, dangling.

Even this *kanaka* get place the sun no go. Aye, right there
in front everybody, his brown winky, winking at all us.

The whole club stay so grossed,
nobody can shoot. Captain Aloha, he
laughing so hard, he like cry. *Braddah*
won the match by default.

So when Captain went pick up the phone: "I, Captain
Aloha," he champs, "Prairie Dog Protector, shall lend
tremendous resources to preserve their environment."

"Yeah, *gunfunnit*," I stay laughing, "you could
*huli* the whole damn colony up your brown winky."

Long time, Captain no say
nothing.

Finally,
"*Braddah*," he says, "my feelings
been insulted."

## Three Mammals Indigenous to Hawai'i
## Before Man's Arrival: The Hawaiian Monk Seal,
## the Hawaiian Bat And Captain Aloha

You got pissed off when the *haole*
wearing one Greenpeace T-shirt asked you if you wanted
for be their poster. Good thing plenty people
Lanikai Beach.

You stroked your Buddha-head, flicked off one stink-eye,
but your beard grinned. Sand funneled down your cut-off
jeans. Whenever you stood for shake 'em out, everybody
near us looked the other way.
                                        A blue-green Samoan
muscle ring tattooed your left arm just under the shoulder.
Construction scars – *Call me the Saw Man* – callused
your thick palms, Popeye forearms.
Least you kept all your fingers.


                                        "Can I go play water,
                                        Daddy," asked Tiny.
                                                You nodded.


How come when one four-year-old baby
weighs hundred twenty pounds, all his buds call
him *Tiny?*
                "Go lie down some more, Captain Aloha,"
                                I said, "I watch him."


Good thing was Tiny woke you, your son
wearing the Greenpeace T-shirt.
*Kolohe* poured water from his plastic bucket
into your jeans.
                "Their skin cannot dry out or they *make,*
                        like die," Tiny shouted, right
                        out of the Discovery Channel.

You jumped up,

                              *Fucka*

almost out your mouth. Now

everybody staring at us.
You think he cared? *Nah*, your son went shove his crotch
at you, grabbed his *ōkole.*
                              "Honk-honk."

                    *Get out my face*, you scolded him.
                    Tiny's thick legs pumping all the way
                                   back to his cousins.

*Braddah, you one sick puppy.*

Must've been cold,
that water. But you never  even wipe off.
Instead you reached
for your shades.
                    *Gotta love 'em, Grey,*
                         biker-beard grinning again.

"Yup, Captain,"

                    Tiny pointed at us, honking his butt.

        "gotta love 'em."

> *If anybody ask, Grey, tell them you*
> *really went try. But like, how many plate*
> *lunches they figured you could eat?*
> Captain Aloha

Kupau:


I made it back to Ft. Collins, still stuffed like one pig.
*Mahalos* plenty for the Elena's lunch, too bad we could
only grind one time together. Yo, you ever ate at Iva's,
behind the Kalihi Diner's, next to the Korean bars?
Go if you never yet.

Braddah John took me there last
Tuesday. When the aunty came for take our order, John
sitting there with his hands crossed on his *opu,* and you
know how thick that stay. Ay, the *hapa-Hawaiian* get his
silver hair in one pony tail, wearing one gold earring and
his Harley jacket. Over sixty now, the *braddah* look *ali'i.*

"Linda, bring the boy whatever he like eat," he
says, "he home little while from Colorado."

And me, so shame. I wearing shorts and tank top cause still
November but after only three days my legs white like your
*ōkole.*

Aunty, she say, "Your uncle told me
all about you, Grey."

Right then, I know stay okay.


So much food. And for broke the mouth, Iva's serves this
*lau-lau* called the *bumbucha.* Captain, I swear the monster
score over two pounds. Get everything inside: pork, one
chicken leg, mahi-mahi and salmon.

*Hala!* My mouth gone home again.

When almost *pau*, Linda comes back, lays down one plate
*haupia* on our table, "Welcome home, Braddah."
    But John, he scold her, "No do that, Aunty."

    But *tita* only wink, "That's why you need for stay home
           more long, Grey."

Horrors, now when she bring us the check, out comes the
*poi* ice cream. "Go try this," puts down the bowl,
two spoons. I already stay stuffed
like one *pua'a* and John diabetic, so all mine
again. The ice cream taste like chalk, no more sugar
or anything but kinda uncool
for give 'em back, yeah?

I went eat almost the whole bowl, Kupau.
        Gotta make face for the aunty.

# *Kao:* Face

### I. Attitude



> *The worst mass murder in state history touches off a massive*
> *manhunt. The suspect surrenders near the Hawai'i Nature*
> *Center. A gunman shot and killed seven people at a Nimitz*
> *Highway office.*
>
> Honolulu Star-Bulletin, *November 2, 1999*

Focus paid off, Byran, bullets
cratering those silhouettes. Nobody had a hope.
Just like any other Tuesday,
you walked in,
      killed seven.

      *What happened, Braddah? They never*
*eat those mangoes you tried for share, laughed*
      *you never go their parties?*

Double-tap: First slow
'em down; second
shot sought their eyes.
      One after another. Your magazine
ran dry, you shoved in one more.   *Snick.*
      *Loose the dogs. But too soon*
     *all gone: never even need your Glock,*
      *high-cap mags.*
      *Only had seven.*

You let Shin slide through, Byran. Mistake.
      *Snick.*

If you coveted number eight,
no more witnesses. Outside that room nobody
even knew
what you done.
      When you walked to your car,
drove to Tantalus, nearest cop was still
half a mile down Nimitz,
in the Zips' parking lot
just Diamond-Head of Xerox.

## Grey Suffers Cultural Displacement Residing in the Foreign Nation of Continental America

Kupau,
Aloha, *Braddah*, how goes it in the homeland? Since I
left the *'ohana* you get one new girlfriend for *wala'au*
with? I no more
nobody for talk to yet. Stay hard. Not like learning for eat
potatoes. Get some others in my workshop, they
try. They like be *local* but no can. They don't know how
for talk Queequeg.
How for drink Moosehead. How for
*pili* me.
You know.


Over here everybody stay so pissed off:
*Keep the fuck out my face*, they say.
You seen 'em in the news? Tied up like one offering.
And the dickheads never even kill him.
Like the goat's head. I no even know
what for say.
What they allow me to say.


At least get one major *local*: "Two Mules for *Sistah* Sarah
Joe." She get two first names, wears boots. After class we
go *wala'au* outside parking lot A. Writes *fuck*
and *futthead* in her poems.
If we was home she could call me "*pake* with
one attitude."


But we stay here.


Sarah Joe get one pretty Golden Retriever
named Blouin. Her fur stay so dark she look almost *'ehu*,
bummers Blouin coming old like Fear. "The clearest
indication of God's lack of omnipotence is the untenable
disparity between the two species' life expectancies."

*All fled, all gone*
*So lift me on the pyre,*
*All our guests have left,*
*And the lamp expires.*

How long you went sit in the Xerox van? Mil-Dot
kissing your cheek, SWAT-Team Captain bull-horned,
*"Bry*an Uyesugi."

You never even hear them
handcuff you,
news-guy taking your picture.

I watched your father on KITV, Byran.
CNN innocence, that's what the reporter figured.
But your daddy, Hiro,
never tell her
what
she wanted:

"I going take one gun
down the police station," he said, "let
my son finish the job."

*After you lost face, I don't*
*know how for find you.*
*Where you stay now?*

"Police Place Uyesugi under 'Suicide-Watch'"
that night. Ten o'clock news,
next morning's *Advertiser*,
everybody
thought they knew.
First-time Hawai'i: Employee
goes "Postal." Not even
that right.
You went Xerox. Copy-Cat
killer,

> *First local, Byran, never before.*
> *You sansei, third generation. No look*
> *away: You one of us.*

other fuck-ups.

> *Nō ka 'oi, braddah.*
> *Number one.*

I kicked Fear when he couldn't hear
me, disobeyed,

                                   *Get out the way,*

purple van
bearing down on him.


                        Driver in the van stopped,
reversed, "Fucker, don't you ever
kick your dog."

                          *No problem, mea culpa.*
                        *Leash the hound. Don't look*
                                    *at haole.*


"You hear me, fucker?" Asshole
drove alongside, "don't look the other way
when I'm talking
to you."
Stopped even with me, "You live
around here?"

                    *"Right there." Point out my house.*
                        *Start walking again.*


Boots got out of the van,
smacked asphalt. "I see you kick your dog
again, I'll break
your ass."

                                      *Huh.*


"You hear me?"
          Approached me,
closed the ten feet.            Not his space.

*Fuck-face now in mine.*

"I fuckin'
ever see you kick your dog
again."

*"Go for it." Release*
*Fear, he growls.*
*Please, please, call*
*me "Chink."*

*Please.*

IV. At Least My Daddy Already Went Die

*With each pass of your hand,*
*you block the light,*
*so my face appears and disappears,*
*appears and disappears.*
Kat's Sister, "Kao-Mise"


Just two of us, Fear and I,
seek breath on Fossil Creek Prairie.
Above
these prairie-dog holes
two hawks cast. One swoops


flesh goes diving. Whistling
surrounds us. I can hear tearing, on the ground raptor's
beak comes up
with sinew.
Bloody carcass half-in, half-out its hole. Second hawk
keeps circling. Fear can't even
sense the young cottontail
bolt ten
feet off his nose,
terrified.


*I stare at your card, Pat.*
*What you wrote when I left home,*
*left the 'ohana.*


Day before workshop all I write
comes up white
space. Rain strikes us,
chop breaks on this reservoir's surface.
No geese honk today. Fear returns to me and we slip
home through the storm.

*You wrote, dear Pat,*
*you poet, my anchor, but three*
*words:*
*"No make shame."*


68

## Notes

1.  The kanji that appears on the back cover of the  book and the section separations represents, according to the  Kenkyusha dictionary, war, rebellion, revolt, insurrection, riot, disturbance. Its meaning starts to get close to the English sense of chaos, as suggested in Kurosawa's movie *Ran*.

2.  *"Kao*: Face,"  epigraph on page 64:  Suicide poem found in the typewriter  of Robert E. Howard, creator of Conan the Barbarian and Kull the Destroyer. In 1936, distressed that his mother would probably not survive her coma, Howard shot himself. His mother died the next day. Funeral services were joint.

## About the Author

Gary Chang was born and raised in Honolulu. His Honors thesis won him the Hemingway Undergraduate Poet of the Year Award from the University of Hawai'i. At  Colorado State University, Fort Collins, he received an MFA in poetry in 2001 while teaching classes in composition and ethnicity. He currently lives in Hawai'i.

## ACKNOWLEDGMENTS

The author would like to thank the editors of the following publications where the following poems first appeared, sometimes in slightly different form.

Online:
*Nieve Roja*: "I Shop Safeway When I Need One Attitude"
*Living Waters*: "*Kao*: Face," "This Aloha We Write One Another," "No Can Find *Wahine*"

Other:
*Hawai'i Review*: "Tiger: An *'Amākua* Feeds," "Lānai After the Pineapple"
*Zaum*: "Under the Winter Moon," "To the Blue-Eyed Gentleman Who Lectured Me About Hegemony While I Played Fetch with Fear"
*Kā Nani*: "Homecoming," "Broken Pies"

In addition, both the author and publisher wish to thank Deborah Woodard for her assistance on this book. *Mahalo*!